THE LITTLE
WHISKY
~ BOOK ~

Susan Fleming

PIATKUS

© 1988 Judy Piatkus (Publishers) Limited

First published in 1988 by
Judy Piatkus (Publishers) Limited,
5 Windmill Street, London W1P 1HF

British Library Cataloguing in Publication Data
Fleming, Susan, *1944–*
The little whisky book.
1. Whiskies
I. Title
641.2′52

ISBN 0-86188-768-9

Drawings by Trevor Newton
Designed by Susan Ryall
Cover photograph by Theo Bergström

Phototypeset in 10 on 11pt Linotron Plantin by
Phoenix Photosetting, Chatham
Printed and bound in Great Britain by
The Bath Press, Avon

CONTENTS

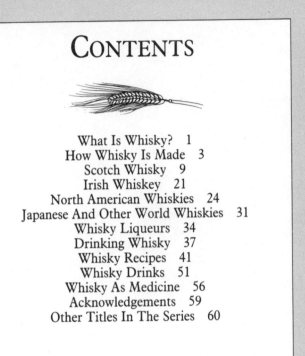

WHAT IS WHISKY?

To a Scotsman, whisky is Glenfiddich, Macallan, Bell's or Teacher's; to an Irishman, it's a Paddy or a Bushmills; to a North American it's a Canadian Club, Jack Daniel's, a bourbon or a rye. To come down to essentials, whisky is a distillate, a spirit produced by the process of distillation (the applying of heat to an alcoholic liquid to extract the alcohol), made from the elements of grain, water and yeast.

Different whiskies are made from different grains: Scotch malt whisky and Irish whiskey contain malted barley, Scotch grain whisky contains barley and corn, and American whiskies rye and corn. Each of these whiskies has its own particular character, dependent not only on the grain or the differing production methods, but on the nature of the water used and even, many believe, on the local climate!

Scotch whisky outsells every other spirit in world markets, and the sheer diversity of single malts and blends has made the name of whisky almost synonymous with Scotch. Scotch whisky is one of Britain's principal and most consistent exports, earning no less than £1,070 million in 1986.

The whiskey of Ireland, where the industry is longer established, is less well known, perhaps, but no less in quality. Both countries are cool and wet, and indeed if it weren't for the weather there would be no whisky. (By the same token, how could the Scots and Irish *bear* the weather if it weren't for the whisky?)

In North America, the distilling skills brought by the Scots and Irish actually caused a 'war' (see page 25) and have resulted in four unique styles of whisky which are becoming very much more internationally known. And in Japan, whisky production cannot keep up with consumption . . .

The name 'whisky' comes from the Gaelic *uisge beatha* or *usquebaugh*, meaning 'water of life' (like the Scandinavian *aquavit* and the French *eau de vie*), and this grain distillate, made for centuries, has become the world's best-selling, best-loved spirit.

How Whisky Is Made

Whiskies the world over are all made in basically the same way.

Malting And Kilning

The grain for malting is soaked in water for two to three days, drained and then allowed to germinate. Each grain will grow a little rootlet of about ⅛ inch (3 mm) long. This renders the starches of the grain more soluble through the action of an enzyme, and will enable the distiller to dissolve out the sugars for fermentation.

After malting, the grain is dried out in kilns and then ground. In Scotland the malt kilns were once entirely peat fed and a proportion of peat is still used, the smoke from this slow-burning fuel giving flavour and colour to the barley.

MASHING

The ground malted barley alone for Scotch malt, or a mixture of malted and cooked unmalted grain (see below) for Scotch grain, Irish and North American whiskies, is next made into a 'porridge' with hot water, and while this infuses the natural conversion of starch into fermentable sugars takes place. The resultant sugary liquid is then drawn off. In all the major whisky-producing countries the solids that remain are processed for use as animal feed.

COOKING

This process is used for unmalted grains. The grain is heated in water so that the starch cells burst, again rendering the sugars more soluble. The cooked grain is combined in a mash with some malted grain, for the enzyme action of the malt.

FERMENTATION

After mashing or cooking the sugary liquid is passed into vast fermentation vessels and yeast is added. The yeast attacks the sugars and converts them into alcohol, a process taking about two days on average. Fermentation can be violent – the vessels often vibrate – and the liquid produced is rather like a strong ale, containing about 10% alcohol.

DISTILLATION

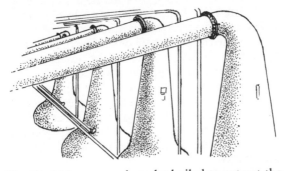

The liquid is now ready to be boiled to extract the alcohol. For Scotch malt and Irish whiskey, this is done in the pot still by the batch method. The huge copper pot stills have a tapering chimney or neck leading to a tube encased in cold water (known as the 'worm'), and it is here that the hot alcoholic steam condenses back into alcohol. This first distillate is impure, crude alcohol, and is passed into another still to be redistilled. The stillman has to judge the precise moment when to 'cut' or collect this second distillation – the first runnings are not considered potable, for instance, nor is the weaker spirit towards the end of distillation. It is a highly skilled job. Irish whiskey and some Scotch malts are then distilled a third time.

The shapes of the pot stills used differ greatly: the very high stills at Glenmorangie are thought to contribute to the whisky's cleanness and lightness, the very small stills at Macallan to its full body. Indeed

Scottish stillmen so value the shapes of their stills that when new stills are to be installed they attempt to recreate every lump and bump of the old ones!

Scotch grain whiskies and American whiskeys are produced in the patent still or Coffey still (invented by Aeneas Coffey, a former Irish exciseman, in 1831), which runs continuously. Hot wash is fed into the top of a first column, the analyser, and steam is fed into the base. As the two meet, the wash boils and the alcohol vapours rise and go down a vapour pipe into the second column, the rectifier. This spirit is very much higher in strength than pot still whisky.

CASKING AND MATURING

Whisky comes from the still at a strength of between 115° and 120° proof (Sikes: see page 8), and this is reduced by adding water before it is put into casks. When Spanish sherry casks were more widely available, before the days of bulk tankers, these were used for maturing Scotch malt whiskies, but most distilleries now use plain or charred oak, or casks which once held bourbon. The sherry and the charring of the wood are thought to impart colour and flavour, but even today the whole chemical process the whisky undergoes during maturation in the cask is imperfectly understood.

The filled casks are stored in warehouses for a minimum of three years in Scotland and Ireland and four years in America (five to fifteen years for the premium brands in all cases). The size of the casks

used, the strength at which the spirit is stored and the temperature and humidity of the warehouses are all important in the maturation. As wood is porous, the whisky 'breathes' during its long storage and this contributes to the mellowing of the fairly raw original spirit. The moistness of the Scottish and Irish climates and the softness of the air are known to be major factors in the success of their whiskies.

As the whisky ages there is a certain amount of evaporation which results in a loss of both volume and strength. One Scotch malt distiller believes he loses the equivalent of 3,000 bottles of whisky a day through this natural evaporation!

After the required maturation time, the whiskies are bottled, or blended and bottled. Water is added to bring the whisky to bottling strength, and often a little caramel to improve colour. This does not affect flavour or strength, despite the belief that the darker a whisky, the stronger. Whisky does not age further in bottle.

PROOF

In 1980, along with other EEC countries, Britain officially adopted the OIML (International Organization of Legal Metrology) system of measurement, replacing the Sikes system used for over 160 years. In Sikes, 100° proof spirit was a mixture of 57.1% spirit and 42.9% water. This meant that a 70° proof whisky – the strength of most whisky sold in bottle – was about 40% alcohol and 60% water by volume. With the OIML system, the conversion is now based on 1 proof gallon (4.55 litres) being equal to 2.595 litres of pure alcohol (that same 57.1%). However, the new system tells us immediately the percentage of alcohol in the whisky: 70° proof (Sikes) is equal to 40° proof (OIML). To further help those who will probably always think of a good malt as 80° proof, most merchants give both old and new measurements on bottle labels.

In the US proof is calculated differently, the 100° proof standard being based on 50% alcohol. The UK 70° proof (Sikes) or 40° proof (OIML) is the equivalent of 80° proof (US) – again, the new system has simplified matters, the US figure being exactly double the OIML.

8

SCOTCH WHISKY

Like Christianity, whisky is thought to have come to Scotland from Ireland. However, the first recorded mention of distilling from malt comes in the Scottish Exchequer Rolls of 1494: 'eight bolls of malt for Friar John Cor wherewith to make *aquae vitae*'.

THE HISTORY OF SCOTCH

Many present-day distilleries in Scotland are located on the sites of ancient pot stills – chosen then as now for the water source, although remoteness from the exciseman was also an important consideration! For the history of Scotch has been bedevilled by conflict between government and distiller. From the beginning of the sixteenth century a series of unpopular licensing laws promoted the growth of illicit stills all over the country, and though a majority were in the inaccessible Highlands, in 1777 there were thought to be some 400 unlicensed (as opposed to eight licensed) stills in Edinburgh alone – even one below the Tron Church in the High Street.

Smuggling the products of the illicit stills became a way of life all over Scotland, and whisky was used as barter. Thousands of gallons were transported in

A Highland illicit still circa 1827

pigs' bladders and tin panniers hidden in women's dresses, in coffins or, more conventionally, in casks on horseback. If they were caught, distillers and smugglers could face transportation.

Although Robert Burns, poet and known whisky imbiber, was himself once an exciseman, he complained bitterly about the taxation on whisky, ending one poem: 'Freedom and whisky gang the gither.' The task that faced the Excise was mammoth: in the year ending July 1824, there were some 3,000 detections of illicit distilling in the single area of Elgin!

It was in this year that the Duke of Gordon, a major Highland landowner, suggested less heavy taxation and a legalising of smaller stills. Ironically, the first person to acquire a licence under the new Whisky Act was George Smith, a tenant of the Duke and a notorious distiller/smuggler whose decision led to much animosity from his former companions in crime. But he prospered, and Smith's Glenlivet – *The* Glenlivet – is one of the finest single malt whiskies.

Legally distilled Scotch whisky was drunk only locally in the early nineteenth century although it had some distinguished 'sassenach' fans. On a state visit to Scotland in 1822 King William IV was presented with some Glenlivet by Sir Peter Grant of Rothiemurchus, MP. His daughter Elizabeth recorded in her memoirs: 'One incident made me very cross. Lord Coryingham, the Chamberlain,

was looking everywhere for the pure Glenlivet whisky; the King drank nothing else. It was not to be had out of the Highlands. My father sent word to me – I was the cellarer – to empty my pet bin, where whisky was long in the wood, mild as milk and the true contraband gout in it.' Sir Walter Scott also shared some whisky with the King on this occasion.

From the mid-nineteenth century onwards, Scotch gradually became more popular outside Scotland and this can be ascribed to three main factors. When Balmoral Castle was built in the early 1850s, Queen Victoria made popular all things Scottish – and she wasn't averse to a dram herself, awarding Royal Warrants to Dewar's and Lochnagar. It is said that on one occasion – absentmindedly, one hopes – she mixed a malt with her claret!

The second factor was the trade agreement entered upon in 1856 by six Lowland patent still distillers who saw a future in the blended whisky which was destined to make Scotch much more accessible to the palates of the English – and the rest of the world. Their association later developed into the great Distillers' Company Limited (DCL) which now owns a huge proportion of the Scotch whisky industry.

The third factor was the phylloxera outbreak which by the 1880s had devastated the French wine and brandy industries. As brandy was *the* drink at the time, a huge gap appeared in the market and Scotch whisky was able to step in and take its place. A whisky boom developed and fortunes were made and lost as distilleries proliferated.

Single malt distillers became increasingly worried about the disproportionate market share held by the blenders, and were delighted when in 1905 Islington Borough Council brought a case against local publicans selling blended whisky. The Council – and ultimately the Courts – said that grain was not genuine whisky but an adulterant of malt. Only after an appeal by DCL was the judgment reversed, in 1908. Whisky was legally defined in 1909, when both grain and malt were deemed to be whisky.

The history of Scotch whisky in the twentieth century is dominated by the crippling duty borne by the industry. In 1900 the duty per gallon (4.5 litres) was 11/- (55p), and in 1987 stood at £4.73 per bottle (£15.77 per litre of pure alcohol). With VAT added, the total tax on a bottle of Scotch is now about £5.70. Thus Scotch, one of Britain's major exports, bears a heavy burden of taxation at home.

MALT WHISKY

Malt whiskies are the cream of the Scotch whisky industry and are divided roughly into four types, by geographical location rather than strictly by style. There are over 100 malt whisky distilleries.

The largest grouping includes all the distilleries north of an imaginary line from Greenock in the west to Dundee in the east. By virtue of numbers these *Highland malts* are the most widely valued; they are smoky smooth with a hint of sherry.

The most famous area is Speyside, with over sixty distilleries, which stretches roughly from Inverness to Aberdeen. The rivers providing the water for the whiskies include the Spey itself plus its tributaries the Livet, Avon, Dullan and Fiddich, as well as the Findhorn, Lossie, Bogie and Deveron.

It is generally acknowledged that the single malts from Glenlivet are the best – and indeed George Smith had to fight a legal battle for the right to call his *The* Glenlivet, when other whiskies appended the prestige of Glenlivet to their names. On the Fiddich is Glenfiddich, the distillery owned by the family company of William Grant and Sons Limited. They have just magnificently celebrated their centenary and the success of their light and smooth single malt which has become the world's biggest seller.

On the Spey itself, the best-known malts are The Macallan, Glenfarclas and Glen Grant (the second most widely distributed single malt after Glenfiddich). North, on the Lossie, is Linkwood – a

manager there refused to have spiders' webs removed in case they might affect the character of the whisky!

In the rest of the region, Glenmorangie is one of the best known and is often compared to a Lowland malt. Highland Park, from the Orkneys, is heavy and powerful and said to be unique in that the water used comes from hidden springs and never sees the light of day. Whisky has been distilled on the Isle of Jura for some 400 years, a proportion illicitly in a cave adjacent to the present distillery (reopened in 1963). Isle of Jura is one of only two malts to be carried on British Airways flights. Talisker, from Skye, is heavily peated and very distinctive.

On the Hebridean island of Islay, just twenty-five miles (forty kilometres) long, are eight distilleries, and the *Islay malts* produced there are the most pungent of all. This is due to the dark, seaweedy, dense-textured peat over which the water flows and to the biting winds, the rain and the sea which batters against the distilleries. Connoisseurs say that

Coal Ila Distillery, Islay in 1953

they can taste iodine or seaweed in Islay malts, particularly the heavier, oilier ones such as Laphroaig and Ardbeg. The other Islay malts are Bruichladdich, Caol Ila, Lagavulin, Bowmore, Bunnahabhain and Port Ellen.

In and around the small town of Campbeltown on the Mull of Kintyre, there used to be thirty-two distilleries. Now there are only two – Springbank and Glen Scotia – and they have not produced whisky for many years. A local coal mine to provide fuel for the stills and huge demand for the full flavour, even saltiness, characteristic of the *Campbeltown malts* contributed to the development of so many distilleries during the whisky boom; cutting corners to supply bootleg whisky to America during Prohibition is said to have been their downfall.

Lowland malts, from distilleries below the imaginary Highland line, are generally lighter, fruitier and sweeter, and many experts suggest that they would provide a gentle introduction to single malts in general. Rosebank is perhaps the best known.

Many more malts than are bottled as singles are

used in blends with grain whiskies, but a few singles are used for vatting – for mixing with other single malts to make a malt-only blend which might appeal to consumers frightened by the power or flavour of a single. Strathconan is the most commonly available of these *vatted malts*. Others are Pride of Islay and Highland Fusilier, said to be bottled especially for the regiment.

GRAIN WHISKIES AND BLENDING

Grain whiskies are distilled by the patent still process, from malted barley and unmalted barley or corn, in distilleries throughout Scotland and all are used in blending. (Old Cameron Brig is the only one available in bottle, a curiosity from the first distiller in the world to make grain whisky.) Grain whiskies are lighter and more neutral in flavour than malts so they are blended with selected malts to achieve a less idiosyncratic whisky that will appeal to a larger market.

Blending is an art and the blender – the 'nose' – will never reveal just what is in his blend. It may include as many as fifty different whiskies with up to 50% malt, though 30% is more usual. In general the higher the proportion of malt, the better the blend.

Some famous blends are Teacher's, Highland Cream, Bell's Extra Special, The Famous Grouse, J&B (light and very popular in the US), Cutty Sark,

Johnnie Walker Red Label (the world's largest-selling whisky) and Black Label, Black & White, White Horse, Haig, Ballantine's, Dewar's, Long John and Whyte & Mackay. A deluxe blend contains a higher proportion of older and therefore more expensive whiskies – Islay Mist, Haig Dimple and Chivas Regal, for instance. Several ages of whisky may be used in a blend, but the age on the label must refer to the youngest of the whiskies.

'Then let us toast John Barleycorn,
Each man a glass in hand;
And may his great prosperity
Ne'er fail in old Scotland!'

John Barleycorn, Robert Burns

Scotch Whisky Traditions

Scotch is the stuff with which the Scot will drink the health of his fellows. With it he will toast the bride – instead of champagne cocktails there are small tumblers of neat whisky at contemporary island weddings. With it he will wet the baby's head – often a Highland new-born is actually given a spoonful. With it he will celebrate Hogmanay – it is the custom even today to see in the New Year by moving from house to house with a bottle (or two) of Scotch to share with friends and neighbours. With it he will bid farewell at funeral wakes – in *Humphry Clinker* Smollett described an Argyllshire funeral from which his hero had retired somewhat prematurely: 'Our entertainer was a little chagrined at our retreat;

and afterwards seemed to think it a disparagement to his family that not above a hundred gallons of whisky had been drank upon such a solemn occasion.' They did better at Flora Macdonald's funeral (she who saved Bonnie Prince Charlie): 3,000 mourners drowned their sorrows in 300 gallons of whisky!

Scotch is also the drink with which to toast the haggis at Burns' Night suppers on 25 January, the anniversary of the poet's birth. Often Scotch is poured over individual helpings as well.

Scotch is the 'cup o'kindness' of *Auld Lang Syne* and plays a restorative role in every part of the Scotsman's life, but on one crucial occasion the magic failed: before Culloden – a major battle lost by the Scots in 1746 – the minister used oatcakes and whisky instead of the Host and consecrated wine.

IRISH WHISKEY

Irish is one of the world's most distinctive whiskey styles; it has a mellow roundness and faint oiliness and, as the kilns use only coal, no hint of smokiness from peat. The whiskeys are distilled three times and are stronger and purer than Scotch.

THE HISTORY OF IRISH WHISKEY

Missionary monks are thought to have brought the secrets of distillation to Ireland in the first century AD and at one time Ireland was the world's largest producer of whiskey.

Sir Walter Raleigh and his queen Elizabeth I (of England *and* Ireland) were both enthusiastic about Irish whiskey but it wasn't until 1608 that Sir

Thomas Phillips, King James's Deputy in Ulster, was allowed to grant licences to distil whiskey. The first he awarded to himself, and Bushmills was founded. Distilleries were licensed in the cities but, as with Scotch, the history of Irish is rich in clashes between government and distillers and illegal pot stills were operated energetically throughout the country. The product was the infamous poteen for which potatoes, other vegetables and fruits were used as well as barley or oats. Rents and tithes were paid in poteen and detections and imprisonments were accepted as part and parcel of rural life. The number of illicit still detections declined during the nineteenth century but poteen continues to be illegally produced in Ireland today and its production may soon be legalised. Even high-rise flats in Belfast are known to emit the fumes!

By 1887 there were twenty-eight legal distilleries in Ireland. A century later all the Irish distilleries merged into Irish Distillers Ltd and there is a huge site at Midleton, near Cork, where almost all the major Irish names are individually produced.

'If his mother had raised him on whiskey, he'd have been a suckling babe to the day of his death.'

Old Irish saying

THE WHISKEYS

Irish whiskeys are pot still whiskeys made from a combination of malted and unmalted barley and other unmalted grains such as oats, wheat and rye. Barley predominates as the moist climate favours its production and indeed malted barley is a major export. Barley also goes to make the famous Irish creamy stouts Guinness, Murphy and Beamish – ideal companions to a tot of whiskey.

In Cork, Paddy is the classic and it gained its name in the twenties through the personality of a salesman, Paddy O'Flaherty. As so many customers asked simply for 'Paddy's whiskey' the principal brand of the Cork Distillers Company was renamed!

From Dublin originally came the classic Irish whiskey – Jameson's. Tullamore Dew originated in Tullamore – named after Daniel E. Williams, the manager, who appended his initials to the name of the town.

The Bushmills Distillery in County Antrim is unusual among Irish producers in that it uses no unmalted barley in its four whiskeys, and Bushmills Malt, marketed since 1984, is Ireland's sole single malt.

NORTH AMERICAN WHISKIES

The whiskeys of the United States are divided basically into three styles – rye, bourbon and the sour mash of Tennessee; Canadian rye whiskies are famous the world over for their lightness.

It wasn't until the arrival of Scots and Irish settlers that whiskey proper began to be made in North America and by the end of the eighteenth century whiskey was *the* drink of the new and expanding nation.

The first whiskeys were distilled from rye in Pennsylvania, Maryland and Virginia, the eastern states where most of the immigrants settled. They were rough spirits produced in homesteads using primitive pot stills and were soon regarded both as a vital medicinal aid and as a form of barter. After the War of Independence the Government realised it could raise revenue from spirits, principally whiskey, and in 1791 instituted taxes as unpopular as those in Scotland and Ireland. Tax collectors were tarred and feathered and events reached a head when General Washington was sent with 13,000 militiamen to quell what came to be known as the 'Whiskey War'. (Washington himself was a major rye whiskey distiller in Virginia and Thomas Jefferson also distilled rye, so two of the first three American presidents were intimately associated with whiskey!)

As a result of this persecution many distillers moved further west and south into the states of Indiana, southern Illinois, Kentucky and Tennessee. Here corn grew well and corn whiskey, and a lighter, mellower style, were born.

The industry began to be rationalised after the introduction of the patent still. One major benefit was the discovery that the spirits were mellower when matured in charred wood, and the 'moonshine' and 'corn likker' of the illicit stills became less popular.

As whiskey continued to grow in popularity so, by the turn of the century, lobbies developed against it: one was religious, one medical and a third was instigated by wives and mothers, a growing number of whom were associated with the suffrage movement. These temperance lobbies led several states to become 'dry' and by 1920, when Prohibition was introduced, thirty-three of the forty-eight had already banned alcohol production and consumption.

For the next thirteen years mayhem followed: fortunes were made by bootleggers – Al Capone among them – and there was probably more liquor available, in the illegal speakeasies, than there ever had been before. Whisky was imported from Canada and Scotland and crude versions were made locally – one such 'Scotch' contained industrial alcohol, caramel, prune juice and creosote! The pot still came back into domestic use and in 1930 a staggering 282,122 illicit stills were discovered.

The public outcry was so great, finally, that in 1933 the Constitution was amended and Prohibition repealed: whiskey became respectable once more. Some states, however, are still dry and the illicit manufacture of whiskey continues to this day.

RYE WHISKEY

Rye whiskey must contain at least 51% rye; other grains included are a fairly large proportion of corn and a small amount of malted barley. Rye must be matured in new charred oak casks for at least four years and is available 'straight' or blended. According to Michael Jackson, author of *The World Guide to Whisky*, rye whiskey has a 'complex, bitter-sweet, fruity, spicy, almost peppermint palate'.

BOURBON

Bourbon, the American classic, must contain at least 51% maize or corn. Maturing is in charred oak barrels, for at least four years but more usually ten or twelve. The longer charred wood maturation that lends bourbon its most significant characteristic, its smooth caramel and vanilla flavour.

Bourbon was first made in and named after Bourbon County, part of Virginia before Kentucky became a separate state. There are no distilleries in Bourbon County now itself but Kentucky is the heart of the bourbon industry and the labels of its best whiskeys proudly proclaim this. The evocative names include Old Grand-Dad, Jim Beam, Early Times and Rebel Yell.

TENNESSEE SOUR MASH WHISKEY

Jack Daniel's old distillery

The whiskey produced in Tennessee is dry and aromatic with a distinct style of its own. Sour mash is used in the production of most American whiskeys (the remnants of mash from which the alcohol has been distilled is returned to the next fermentation) and the unique style of Tennessee comes rather from the filtration of the distilled whiskey through thick piles of finely ground sugar maple charcoal, a process which can take up to ten days and which leaches all impurities out of the whiskey. In Scotch this might also leach out taste but in a whiskey such as Jack Daniel's it is said to *add* a faint smoky flavour.

And it is Jack Daniel's of Lynchburg – the 'sippin' whiskey' – that is the classic of Tennessee. Jack Daniel is said to have been thirteen years old when he started distilling and nineteen when he set up his own distillery. Ironically Moore County, of which Lynchburg is the county seat, is dry; the distillery may manufacture and ship whiskey but the retail sale is illegal.

CANADIAN WHISKY

Like American whiskey, Canadian whisky originated with Scots and Irish immigrants. It is made by a
process similar to rye or bourbon, principally from
malted and unmalted rye, with some corn. All Canadian whiskies are blended with neutral grain spirits
and contain less than 10% of the straight spirit.
They are made by the patent still process, distilled
several times and matured in charred or uncharred
new wood for between four and twelve (or more)
years before being blended (from up to fifty
whiskies). The characteristic cleanness and lightness of Canadian whiskies have given them a
distinctive style of their own and Canada is an
extremely influential force in the world's whisky
industry.

By the 1840s there were about 200 distilleries in
Canada, mainly along the banks of the St Lawrence
river and on the shores of the Great Lakes. Among
them were two companies which today dominate the
local industry and indeed the world – Seagram's and

Hiram Walker – both of which flourished during Prohibition.

After the repeal of Prohibition, Seagram's – headed by a giant of the industry, Samuel Bronfman – launched their whiskies in the US. Brands include Crown Royal (created to honour King George VI when he visited Canada in 1939), VO, Five Star and Hudson's Bay Special. By the 1970s Seagram's were the largest distilling group in the world: they own eight Speyside malts, among them The Glenlivet, and a bestseller is the deluxe blend Chivas Regal. They also own Mumm's champagne and have recently acquired Martell, the French cognac.

Hiram Walker, whose ancestors were English, launched his famous Canadian Club in 1884. The company has substantial holdings in Scotland and also owns Kahlua, the Mexican coffee liqueur.

> 'Four and twenty Yankees
> Feeling mighty dry
> Took a trip to Canada
> And bought a case of rye.
> When the case was opened,
> The Yanks began to sing
> "To hell with the President,
> God save the King!" '

JAPANESE AND OTHER WORLD WHISKIES

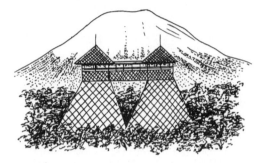

On 11 December 1987 the MP for Tayside North spiritedly argued in the British House of Commons that the name of whisky should be protected as the name of champagne had been since 1934. Scotch whisky has been *defined* since 1909 but now that it is exported not only in bottles but in bulk to the world its reputation could be in great danger. Many countries that import Scotch in bulk blend it with locally produced grain spirit and market the result as whisky; many also label this spurious blend as 'Scotch' and the crusade against this practice keeps The Scotch Whisky Association considerably occupied. In the case of Japan, which in 1986 bought 51% of the bulk malt exported from Scot-

land, their own high-quality whiskies are accented with a Scotch malt, but many countries are not so scrupulous and the good name of whisky, especially Scotch, is thought by many to be at risk.

JAPANESE WHISKY

The Japanese consumption of whisky is second only to that of the USA. They import vast quantities of Scotch whisky, have interests in the Scottish industry and also manufacture their own. Indeed Japanese whisky is generally acknowledged to be one of the world's five styles of quality whisky.

The first Japanese distillery was founded by Shin-jiro Torii in 1923 and grew into the massive Suntory – perhaps best known in the UK for its sponsorship of golf, another Scottish export which the Japanese embraced with enthusiasm. Other whisky companies are Nikka, Sanraku Ocean and Kirin Seagram.

In general style Japanese whiskies are closely related to those of Scotland although they are less peaty. They are made similarly, by both pot still and patent still processes, using local peat and pure, clean water (Kirin Seagram's water comes from Mount Fuji), and maturation takes place in sherry, bourbon or new charred oak casks.

OTHER WHISKIES

Australian whisky has been distilled in Victoria since 1866 but it wasn't until after World War I that the business began seriously. Now there are several major malt and grain blends, roughly in the Scottish manner. New Zealand has been making bourbon-style whiskey since 1969.

WHISKY LIQUEURS

L iqueurs are sweetened wines or spirits flavoured with aromatics – fruits, herbs, beans or kernels. The purest spirits make the finest liqueurs and there are many with a whisky base. Most can be drunk at any time, straight or 'on the rocks', but are probably best after dinner. Many can be used in cooking as well.

SCOTCH WHISKY LIQUEURS

The king of them all is Drambuie, at least 200 years old, which uses both malt and grain whiskies, heather honey, herbs and other secret ingredients. The name is a corruption of *an dram buidheach*, Gaelic for 'the dram that satisfies'. It is made in Skye and legends abound concerning its sub-title, 'Prince Charles Edward's Liqueur'. In recognition of the bravery that carried him 'over the sea to Skye' Bonnie Prince Charlie is said to have given the Mackinnons of Skye the recipe. The company still market it and launched another liqueur, Scotch Apple, in the 1980s.

Glen Mist is the second oldest Scotch whisky liqueur and during World War II it emigrated to Eire where it was made with Irish whiskey. Glen Mist is now produced in Scotland again and has left its progeny, Irish Mist, in Ireland.

Other Scotch liqueurs are Glayva, Clanrana, Lochan Ora, Sconie, and two made with cream, Alexander's and Columba Cream. Redalevn (Red Eleven), a dry Scotch liqueur, was created especially for the footballers of Manchester United!

> 'Ma wee laud's a sojer;
> He works in Maryhill;
> He gets his pay on a Friday night,
> And buys a hauf-a-gill.
> Goes to church on Sunday
> Hauf-an-hoor too late;
> He pu's the buttons aff his shirt,
> An' pits them in the plate.'
>
> Glasgow street song

IRISH WHISKEY LIQUEURS

Irish Mist is the Irish version of Glen Mist and Irish Velvet is a bottled version of Irish coffee (see page 53), produced by Jameson's. Other Irish liqueurs are Snug, Mulligan's and Gallwey's. Bailey's Irish Cream, launched in 1974, blends cream and Irish and is the best-selling liqueur in the world; a host of similar liqueurs are also produced locally.

AMERICAN WHISKEY LIQUEURS

Southern Comfort, bourbon-based with peaches, oranges and herbs, is the most familiar. It is also made under licence in Eire. Another bourbon-based liqueur is Wild Turkey which contains honey and citrus flavours.

DRINKING WHISKY

Whisky can be drunk at any hour and many a distillery worker in Scotland takes a wee dram to start the day. In fact professional tasters confirm that the best time for tasting is the morning when the palate is still fresh.

For the amateur, though, Scotch should perhaps be kept for later in the day: before dinner as an aperitif, or after as a digestif. Generally speaking Scotch blends or the lighter malts could be taken before and the more characterful malts afterwards instead of brandy or liqueur. On one occasion in 1954, historic both for Britain and for the Scotch malt industry, a Macallan was offered to Kruschev and Bulganin as an alternative to the usual cognac after a Mansion House dinner.

Dilution of Scotch is a matter of taste. Purists say that the best water to use is that from which the Scotch was made, but as this is well nigh impossible for all but a few lucky locals a still, bottled spring water would be the best alternative. Purists also condemn the use of ice, ginger ale or soda but, curiously, many Scots drink their blends with lemonade. A little water added to a good malt can help bring out its full flavour while Lagavulin recommend the use of unchilled water in a 50:50 dilution. Generally speaking a pre-prandial whisky could be diluted, a post-prandial malt drunk neat.

In Scottish pubs – until comparatively recently male preserves – a Scotch is chased down with a half pint of beer ('a hauf and a hauf'). The Irish do this too, accompanying an Irish with a pint of local stout. More usually, however, Irish is offered straight or neat, without ice, but with a jug or glass of water for personal dilution if desired – rarely more than 50:50.

Bourbon drinkers take it straight or with a little 'branch water' – local stream water again, ideally – and without ice (something of an oddity in America). Purists again say there should be no dilution with soda or ginger ale but the Americans are past masters at 'disguising' spirits – a skill acquired during Prohibition when they invented the cocktail.

The Japanese dilute their whisky more than anyone else, with up to four parts water, and a Japanese word meaning 'diluted with water' has virtually become the name for an after-work whisky.

WHISKY-DRINKING TERMS AND MEASURES

Briefly, the names of measures of whisky in Scotland and the US deserve some examination. The traditional and colloquial words in Scotland are 'tot', 'dram', 'nip' and 'spot'. All these words are *small* in quantity, and are usually further qualified by 'wee' – 'a wee nip'; the Scots *do* have a fondness for the diminutive but it's probably more to do with the well-known Scottish habit of understatement!

The Americans, on the other hand, have a whiskey vocabulary which is rather aggressive and *fast*. The land of the supposed 'sippin' whiskey' uses words such as 'snort', 'belt', 'shot', 'blast' and 'slug', all evocative of the cowpoke knocking back a glassful in one!

The Americans are, appropriately, more munificent than any other nation with their whiskey, selling it in 'fingers' – the height of two fingers held horizontally across the glass makes a measure of at least 2 fl oz (50 ml). The British are parsimonious by comparison, serving ⅙ gill (⅚ fl oz or about 20 ml) in England or ⅕ gill (1 fl oz or about 25 ml) in Scotland.

WHISKY GLASSES

Whisky can be drunk from anything. Blenders use tulip-shaped glasses and a good after-dinner malt might be served thus. Bourbon ought to be drunk from a large tumbler, Irish from a smaller tumbler and whisky cocktails in glasses designated variously Collins, highball, lowball, old-fashioned, Martini or sour. Mint juleps should, of course, be drunk from silver mugs.

The shape of the container really makes no appreciable difference to the drink, however – it's merely a matter of custom.

'There are two things a Scotsman likes naked, and one is malt whisky.'

Scottish proverb

WHISKY RECIPES

Whisky can in theory be used in any recipe that calls for alcohol and will add its own unique flavour. Instead of brandy, whisky of any type could be added to cake mixtures, marmalade, Christmas puddings and mincemeat. It could be used to flame meat and fish dishes – and there is no reason why Crêpes Suzette should not be transformed: Crêpes Morag, Bridie or Peggy-Sue, perhaps?

A breakfast porridge could be topped with butter and malt whisky, and Scotch Broth is traditionally spiked with a wee dram of the hard stuff. Fruit could be preserved in whisky. Think, too, about using whisky or whisky liqueurs in dessert sauces, over ice cream or cakes, in sweet soufflés, syllabubs and mousses or in home-made liqueur chocolates.

CHICKEN LIVER WHISKY PÂTÉ

Any pâté recipe which specifies a touch of brandy or other alcohol could be laced with whisky instead.

3 oz (75 g) butter
1 onion, peeled and finely chopped
1 large garlic clove, peeled and crushed
1½ lb (675 g) chicken livers, well trimmed
salt
freshly ground black pepper
1 tablespoon double cream
2 level tablespoons tomato paste
3 tablespoons malt whisky

Melt the butter in a pan and fry the onion and garlic until transparent. Add the livers and fry for about 5–7 minutes (they should still be pink inside). Remove from the heat and add the remaining ingredients.

Purée in a blender, then pass through a sieve into a bowl. Chill until required.

Serves 8–10

POACHED MONKFISH WITH WHISKY SAUCE

This recipe is adapted from one issued by The Scotch Malt Whisky Society. First of all, make a good flavourful, reduced fish stock in which to poach the monkfish, and add a tablespoon of malt whisky.

4 monkfish fillets, about 1½ lb (675 g) total weight
½ pint (300 ml) good fish stock (see above)
4 fl oz (120 ml) double cream
2 tablespoons malt whisky
salt
freshly ground black pepper
4 dill sprigs

Poach the fish in the stock for about 10 minutes, or until just cooked. Drain the fish (reserve the poaching stock), transfer to a serving dish and keep warm while you prepare the sauce.

Pour just over half the stock into a clean saucepan and add the cream and half the whisky. Heat gently, without boiling, for about 5 minutes. Season to taste and add the remaining whisky, then pour the sauce over the fish. Serve garnished with the dill.

Serves 4

GAELIC STEAKS

This recipe is courtesy of The Glenlivet. A steak could also be flamed with whisky.

4 fillet steaks
freshly ground black pepper
1 tablespoon vegetable oil
1 oz (25 g) butter
salt
4 tablespoons The Glenlivet

Season the steaks on both sides with plenty of black pepper. Heat the oil and butter in a frying pan and fry the steaks for 2–5 minutes, depending on how well you want them done. Place on a hot serving dish and sprinkle with salt.

Pour the whisky into the frying pan and heat through gently with the meat juices to make a sauce. Pour over the steaks and serve at once.

Serves 4

CRANACHAN

Cranachan, a traditional Scottish dessert, can also be made using crowdie, a Highland cream cheese, instead of cream. An even simpler version comes from Skye: just give everyone his or her own bowl of whipped cream, and let them help themselves to toasted oatmeal, Talisker (of course) and sugar to taste.

4 tablespoons medium oatmeal
1 pint (600 ml) double or whipping cream
sugar or heather honey
2 tablespoons (or more) malt whisky
fresh loganberries or raspberries (optional)

Toast the oatmeal and set it aside to cool. Whip the cream until frothy, adding sugar or honey to taste and the whisky. Mix the oatmeal into the cream, and serve with the loganberries or raspberries, if you like.

Serves 4–8

GINGER AND WHISKY ICE CREAM

This recipe is from The Scotch Malt Whisky Society. It is a particularly happy marriage of alcohol and ice cream – a Whisky Mac ice cream, virtually!

4 egg yolks
3 oz (75 g) caster sugar
¾ pint (450 ml) milk
1 teaspoon ground ginger
2 tablespoons malt whisky
¼ pint (150 ml) double or whipping cream
3 oz (75 g) crystallised or stem ginger, finely chopped

Beat the egg yolks and sugar together in a large bowl until thick and pale yellow in colour. Put the milk and ground ginger into a saucepan and bring to a simmer, then very gradually pour the hot milk on to the egg yolks, stirring constantly. Strain the mixture into the top of a double saucepan and stir over a gentle heat until the custard thickens enough to coat the back of a wooden spoon. Do not allow to boil. Pour into a large mixing bowl and allow to cool, then add the whisky.

Beat the cream until it forms soft peaks, then fold it into the custard. If you are using an ice cream machine, add the crystallised ginger and freeze; if using a domestic freezer, freeze for 1 hour, then beat in the ginger and refreeze.

Serves 4

BOURBON PECAN TART

A typical and rich American pie, this recipe could be adapted using other nuts and other whiskies.

1 pâté brisée flan case, baked blind until golden in a
loose-bottomed 10 inch (25 cm) flan tin
2 eggs
12 oz (350 g) golden syrup
5 oz (150 g) dark brown sugar
1 tablespoon melted unsalted butter
2 tablespoons bourbon
¾ teaspoon vanilla essence
5–6 oz (150–175 g) pecan nuts, coarsely chopped

Let the flan case cool in the tin while you make the filling. Put the eggs, syrup and sugar in a bowl and beat until well combined. Stir in the remaining ingredients.

Spoon into the flan case and bake in a preheated oven at 350°F/180°C/Gas 4 for 20–25 minutes or until the centre is firm. Cool on a rack before removing from the tin.

'He is a gentleman, a scholar and a judge of good whiskey.'

American folk saying

HOOTENHOLLER WHISKEY CAKE

A traditional cake from Georgia.

4 oz (100 g) butter
7 oz (200 g) caster sugar
3 eggs
4 oz (100 g) plain flour, sifted
1/2 teaspoon baking powder
1/2 teaspoon grated nutmeg
1/4 teaspoon salt
4 tablespoons milk
3 oz (75 g) black treacle
1/4 teaspoon bicarbonate of soda
1 lb (450 g) raisins
10 oz (275 g) pecan nuts, chopped
2 fl oz (60 ml) bourbon

Cream together the butter and sugar, then beat in the eggs. Sift the flour again with the baking powder, nutmeg and salt, and add to the eggs a tablespoon at a time, alternating with the milk. Mix together the treacle and bicarbonate of soda and add to the batter along with the remaining ingredients.

Pour into a greased and lined 3–4 lb (1.3–1.8 kg) cake or bread tin and bake in a preheated oven at 300°F/150°C/Gas 2 for about 2 hours. (A fine skewer inserted in the centre will come out clean when the cake is done.)

BOURBON PEACHES

Adapted from *The New England Heritage Cookbook* by Jean Hewitt, quoted in *Preserving* (Time-Life Books). Many other fruits could be preserved in a similar way.

2¼ lb (1 kg) sugar
9 fl oz (250 ml) water
6 inch (15 cm) cinnamon stick, broken
½ tablespoon whole cloves
2¼ lb (1 kg) ripe peaches, scalded and peeled
¾ pint (450 ml) bourbon

In a large pan, dissolve the sugar in the water over a low heat. Tie the cinnamon and cloves in a muslin bag and add them to the pan. Bring this sugar syrup to the boil. When the syrup is clear, add the peaches, a few at a time, and simmer for about 5 minutes, until they are barely tender. Do not overcook. Remove the peaches from the syrup and set them aside to drain well. Repeat until all the peaches are cooked, then boil the syrup until it is slightly thickened (222°F or 105°C on a sugar thermometer). Cool slightly.

Stir the bourbon into the syrup. As the peaches drain, place them in hot, sterilised jars. Cover them with the bourbon syrup, then seal and store in a cool, dark, dry place.

WHISKY TRUFFLES

Use bourbon, Scotch malt, Irish, Drambuie or Southern Comfort for differing luxurious flavours.

12 oz (350 g) good dark chocolate
1 oz (25 g) unsalted butter
¼ pint (150 ml) double cream
12 tablespoons whisky or liqueur
cocoa powder
icing sugar

Melt the chocolate and butter together in a double saucepan, then leave to cool. Mix in the cream and the alcohol, and chill until malleable.

Dust the work surface with equal quantities of cocoa and icing sugar and roll the paste into a sausage shape. Cut off small pieces and roll into balls. Dust with more cocoa and icing sugar.

Whisky Drinks

Hot Toddy

A whisky toddy was a common drink in eighteenth-century Scotland, and contained simply whisky, sugar and hot water. Having a cold is as good an excuse as any . . .

Put a tablespoon of a blended whisky into a mug, add runny honey to taste and some fresh lemon juice, and fill the mug with hot water. Stir well.

Atholl Brose

Named after a Duke of Atholl, this is a mixture consumed enthusiastically at Hogmanay.

6 oz (175 g) medium oatmeal
½ pint (300 ml) water
3 tablespoons heather honey
about 750 ml (1¼ pints) blended whisky

Put the oatmeal into a bowl and mix with the water to a thick paste. Leave for an hour, then strain through a fine sieve. Press the oatmeal until it is quite dry and then discard.

Mix the cloudy liquid with the honey, pour into a large bottle and fill up with whisky. Shake well before use.

HET PINT

An aromatic drink made up hot for the 'first fits' –
the first people to set foot through the doors after the
New Year has begun.

4 pints (2.25 litres) mild ale
1 teaspoon grated nutmeg
sugar to taste
3 eggs
½ pint (300 ml) blended whisky

Put the ale in a large pan, add the nutmeg and sugar
to taste, and simmer until the sugar has melted.

Beat the eggs in a separate container and pour a
little of the hot liquid on to them. Mix well and
strain back into the bulk of the ale. Add the whisky
and heat again – do this gently, otherwise the eggs
will curdle.

WHISKY MAC

This should perhaps be made with a blend that uses Balmenach, a Highland malt owned by John Crabbie, famous for its green ginger wine. Simply mix 2 measures of Scotch and 2 of ginger wine.

IRISH COFFEE

This is said to have been invented in 1952 at Shannon Airport where planes used to refuel before crossing the Atlantic. One cold night the barman there made a warming coffee and whiskey drink for an American newspaperman. He introduced it to his favourite bar, the Buena Vista in San Francisco, where half a million Irish coffees are now sold every year.

Warm a stemmed glass slightly and pour in some hot, freshly made coffee. Dissolve sugar to taste in this, then pour in a measure of Irish. Pour on some runny or lightly whipped cream over the back of a spoon and serve immediately.

HIGHLAND COFFEE

Simply use Scotch instead of Irish as above.

Raspberry Cordial

This recipe comes from a book called *Seventy-five Receipts*, published in America in 1838.

'To each quart of raspberries allow a pound of loaf-sugar. Mash the raspberries and strew the sugar over them, having first pounded it slightly or cracked it with a rolling pin. Let the raspberries and sugar sit till the next day, keeping them well covered, then put them in a thin linen bag and squeeze out all the juice with your hands. To every pint of juice, allow a quart of double-rectified whiskey. Cork it well and set it away for use. It will be ready in a few days.'

Old-Fashioned

Put a cube of sugar into the bottom of an old-fashioned glass (American cocktail jargon for a squat tumbler) and shake 2 drops of Angostura bitters on top. Crush together. Add 2–3 ice cubes, and pour in a measure of bourbon or rye. Garnish with a twist of lemon peel and a Maraschino cherry, if you like.

MANHATTAN

Put 4–5 ice cubes into a jug, and pour in 1 part sweet Italian vermouth and 3 parts rye or bourbon. Stir vigorously and pour into a chilled martini glass. Garnish with a cherry.

WHISKEY SOUR

Simply shake 2 parts bourbon or rye, the juice of ½ lemon and ½ teaspoon sugar with some crushed ice.

Topped with soda water and garnished with fresh fruit, it is transformed into a Tom Collins or John Collins.

TENNESSEE MINT JULEP

Put 6 sprigs of fresh young mint into an iced mug or glass, add 1 teaspoon sugar syrup, and crush together. Pack the mug or glass with crushed ice and pour in bourbon to the top. Stir, then garnish with 3 more mint sprigs. Drink through a straw.

A julep could be made with Southern Comfort instead of bourbon, but perhaps leaving out the syrup.

Whisky As Medicine

In the Middle Ages, spirits were regarded as a cure for many ailments and Holinshed, author of *The Chronicles of England, Scotland and Ireland* (which Shakespeare 'distilled' to such great effect), was particularly in favour of *uisge beatha*: 'beying moderately taken' it not only retards aging and banishes melancholy, but it 'preserveth the head from whyrling, the eyes from dazelying, the tongue from chatterying, the throte from ratlying . . . truly it is a soveraigne liquor if it be orderlie taken'. A testimonial indeed, but if taken in a *dis*orderly fashion, the opposite would be the case!

In *Humphry Clinker* (1771) Smollett, too, referred to whisky's medicinal qualities: the Scots 'find it an excellent preservative against the winter cold . . . I am told that it is given with great success to infants, as a cordial . . .' And it was in Edinburgh's famous

Rose Street that poet James Hogg (the 'Ettrick Shepherd') was said to have pronounced on the therapeutic qualities of The Glenlivet: 'If a body could just find oot the exac' proportion and quantity that ought to be drunk every day, and keep to that, I verily trow that he might leeve for ever, without dyin' at a', and that doctors and kirkyards would go oot o' fashion.'

Later, whiskies in Scotland and Ireland were advertised as actively promoting health: an 1887 claim for a Dublin whiskey bore an endorsement from the *British Medical Journal* and one Scotch company marketed a grain whisky for diabetics. In Ireland, to rid their hands of the aches and pains concomitant with picking potatoes, poteen manufacturers would rub in their product nightly.

In America the claims were no less insistent and indeed whiskey was often the only medicine available to the frontiersman. It was used as a disinfectant to sterilise water and wounds and in *The Mother's Book of Daily Duties* of 1855 there is a recipe for chill and fever: 'Take 3 cents worth of garlic and ½ pint of rye whiskey, put them in a bottle and take a tablespoonful (for an adult) at night.'

Neat whisky is still a good gargle for a sore throat, having an anaethetising affect, but the claim that it cures colds is probably more due to the sufferer *feeling* better after a whisky!

As recently as 1984 the British claims were still flying. Lord Boothby asked the Government whether it realised that 'Scotch whisky is about the only thing left that brings guaranteed comfort to mankind'. He was supported by Lord Shinwell who thought Scotch should be available on the National Health and that it should be a legitimate expense for the Lords 'since there is a general consumption of this liquid by noble Lords, and since many of them cannot do without it because it is in the nature of a medicine'. As Lord Shinwell saw his own centenary it surely must be true that 'beying moderately taken' whisky can indeed be regarded as the 'water of life' and one of life's greatest pleasures.

ACKNOWLEDGEMENTS

Thanks are due to the following: Jack Daniel's, The Glenlivet (Seagram's), The Scotch Malt Whisky Society, The Scotch Whisky Association, John Tovey, and especially William Grant & Sons Ltd and Isle of Jura distillery (The Invergordon Distillers Ltd) for enabling some first-hand gustatory research.

The two seminal works on whisky are *The World Book of Whisky* by Brian Murphy (Collins, 1978) and *The World Guide to Whisky* by Michael Jackson (Dorling Kindersley, 1987). All Derek Cooper's writings on Scotch are entertaining and packed with information, as is David Daiches' *Scotch Whisky* (André Deutsch, 1969).

The Scotch Whisky Association, 20 Atholl Crescent, Edinburgh, produce a map of the Scotch whisky distilleries and much information on the industry. The Scottish Tourist Board, 22 Ravelston Terrace, Edinburgh, have a map of the only 'malt whisky trail' in the world (encompassing Strathisla, Glenfiddich, Tamnavulin, The Glenlivet, Glenfarclas, Tamdhu and Glen Grant). The Scotch Malt Whisky Society promote malts (obviously) but also make available their own bottlings of unique malts straight from cask; they are at 87 Giles Street, Edinburgh.